WHAT ARE YOU?

Not this person you think you are

Sebastian Lyall

I believe there is something going on in a conscious being, which includes many animals, as well as ourselves, that is not a computational activity. And to be conscious at all is not a quality that a computer as such will ever possess - no matter how complicated, no matter how well it plays chess or any of these things.

Roger Penrose
Nobel Prize Winner 2020

I thank everything that has
happened to me.

Everything & everyone.

Introduction
&
Background

My name is Sebastian, however, I am not Sebastian "the personality". I think I am Sebastian and everyone who meets me thinks I am Sebastian. That makes me Sebastian in this world. However, it is purely by our brains' imagination and perception that Sebastian exists as a personality in each of our minds. This personality is a collection of thoughts, memories and experiences gathered over time.

If this person Sebastian is a totally different personality in each of our brains, based on their own perspective and experience of him, then what am I?

Is there a personality in reality out there or is it all experienced in the mind? What is the nature of the experiencer of life? If my knowing, which is essentially what I mean when I say "I am", has been here throughout the life of Sebastian and I have experienced the change in his life, then what is my nature? Why are we here and why is there pain and suffering?

These questions have been addressed by thinkers, writers, prophets, artists, poets, teachers, leaders and people from all walks of life in every generation. I am sure you have thought about these as well. What is life and what is its purpose? How can we end continuous seeking and suffering in a society more abundant in wealth and technology than ever? Health crises, inflation, climate crises, mass migration, wars, food supply and poverty are only some of the problems we are collectively facing today. So we ask ourselves, is there another way humans can survive? Is there another way to live?

It is time to dive into this question and discover our true nature, as that is where answers to all questions live. It is also where peace, harmony and absolute joy reside. It is time to understand what we really are and what is the nature of reality which we experience; which is very different from what we have been programmed to see and understand.

From the day we are born, whoever we are, our minds are programmed to act and behave in certain ways. These ways (culture, climate, history, society, family, laws and so on...) create memories, habits, preferences and all other known "human" phenomena. In this process, there is one memory or programming which trumps them all, and it is reinforced daily. It is a "fact" that your brain never really forgets and it is your name, identity and your perceived personality and that you exist as a limited and finite human being. It is the idea of who you are and it lives as the strongest energy flow in your brain. Hence what you consider "you", is a direct result of data, events and memories. These events are always happening and in constant flux of change, for example, the Sebastian we know is constantly changing. Every human's life swings between happiness and sadness, pain and pleasure and other such dualistic and cyclical phenomenon.

Due to the highly programmed nature of our minds, we end up thinking we are constantly changing and evolving. That however is not true from your own experience of life. Yes, your personality is constantly changing, but that is not you. You are the knowing of this change hence you don't change with this movement of life. If our brains and bodies are dynamic and constantly evolving, we can't be that. Simply because we are observing all these changes. We are not our thoughts and sensations themselves, we are the one that is aware of them.

Observe and you will realise that your thoughts changed in the last 15 minutes, which means you can't be in them. Imagine the act of watching cars pass by; you are clearly not in the cars, and in the same way, if the movement of thoughts can be observed, then you are not the movement itself.

Stillness needs to exist to observe any movement.

If we are unchanging, then what are we? You are akin to a still point, hence you can experience the movement of thought. Your existence and presence, and hence you, has nothing really to do with the autonomous and perpetual movement of thoughts.

So, if you are not your changing thoughts or memories, which are stored as neural pathways in the brain, then what is our nature and what do you do about this information?

We surely can't be a mere energy flow in the brain which generates thoughts. The question is not really about who we are but essentially about "what" we are. What is the nature of the being which is experiencing the taste of coffee and the love for their mother? What are we doing in the human body and mind? What is our role here in this world and in life? How does this human design work? How do the brain and body make decisions and what does that mean for us?

This book speaks of my experience of life and consists of my realisations and questions I ask, enabling the exploration and the journey into our true self, but above all, it is about detaching yourself from your data-driven mind and calorie-loaded body so you can experience life without any conditioning and limiting subjectivity of your past.

Together, we will discuss the truth which has been hidden in plain sight from all of us. In a messy and unhappy world, for many, it is a relief to realise that there is another force of life within them. It is a relief for them to discover this truth.

My realisation took a few years and I don't wish the pain I had to go through on anyone. However, I do wish everyone the experience and understanding of life which came as a result of it.

After a botched gut surgery in 2018 that wrecked my life, put me in a hospital for months and led to countless other procedures, excruciating neurological pain, alcoholism, clinical depression and two suicide attempts, something happened to me that changed the very core of my beliefs about reality, consciousness and who we really are.

On a small beach, alone in Thailand, I experienced a phenomenon which I couldn't have explained at the time.

Exercising and stretching on a hot day at the beach was a habit I had. Perhaps because I felt good or perhaps my mind had seen all of those videos of people doing it. This time I was very relaxed and at peace, as I had left London and my hectic work for a couple of weeks and was on the serene island of Koh Phangan.

I had eaten well for the last few months, stopped drinking and exercised regularly and the sun made me feel happier and relaxed. Let's just say my brain was on my side and not overly occupied with all the stimulation experienced in a big city and entrepreneurship.

On that day, while in the child's pose, I vanished into the realm of existence without the experience of life. The movie of life totally stopped playing and my body and mind vanished for hours. There was a sense of presence and knowing of sorts which is impossible to explain. My brain and body went numb and I felt as if I had rested for a thousand years in a few hours, Time really wasn't an object in this space and when Sebastian (the person I thought I was) came back to life, he experienced a convergence of all universal objects and possible experiences into a single dot which was within him. My brain saw everything humans can possibly experience converge into some sort of place inside me. The sun, the stars, the moon, the galaxies, childbirth, rain, sexual experiences, death and life - all of it.

This can sound like a cliché but this experience happens to humans all over the world. Eckhart Tolle and J Krishnamurti are amongst some who had similar experiences spontaneously. This experience can be characterised as a spiritual awakening, a psychological transformation, and a reconditioning of the mind.

In short, my brain saw me, the experiencer of life and recognised it.

The second realisation came as soon as my eyes opened and this body and mind came back to life. In an instant, my brain saw the world being projected out from that single source of information, which was also the destination of all experiences as well.

It was only a few weeks later that I realised that my brain, totally and completely, understood the nature of reality after seeing it first-hand. It saw something so vividly real that it couldn't unsee it.

I realised all that I see originates from me and also ends in me, hence all my life experience is a world I built in my brain. There was also an instant recognition between the thinking and the knower of that thinking; of the separation of perception of life and the perceiver of life.

I woke up shaking, sweating and with lots of froth in my mouth. I knew I saw something but at that time, I had no understanding of what had happened.

It is indeed hard to understand with perceptive thought and even harder to explain with our limited and dualistic language. I realised the story in my brain was running like a movie which I was here to watch.

It was a realisation that, in life, one is only essentially experiencing oneself and all this experience is happening internally, in one's own body and mind.

I also realised that this experience was not limited to my own being, but that it was also present in what was being observed.

It felt as if my brain's source of information and programming was changed from external knowledge, books or society, to the internal and eternal knowledge of our own being; the oneself.

What I thought was only a few minutes of a meditative state, was actually hours long as the mind had stopped registering the idea of time. Unknown to me at that time, I had experienced something we humans call "awakening"

I would come to realise later that I had an awakening called Nirvilapka Samadhi in Hinduism or Nirvana in Buddhism. I had never heard of these concepts in this context but only that Nirvana was a very famous rock band! As a serial entrepreneur, my awakened state has always been when my mind is thinking and planning - quite the opposite of what the word means.

This experience however changed Sebastian's life. In the next couple of weeks, he would get rid of seven pills including two antidepressants, Ritalin, and two nerve painkillers from his daily routine. He got rid of his sciatica and insomnia and started eating healthy and exercising. He had a different glow and vigour for life and suddenly everything looked and felt beautiful. This was all happening by itself and he was no longer sad and his brain was clear and sharp. He cured his clinically diagnosed depression and neurological pain and it felt as if he was given a new life. A new chance after searching for health all over the world for 6 years.

Everything suddenly was just fine. I looked at everything from a different set of eyes and very soon the concept and idea of right and wrong were thrown out of my

There is only one way out of all the pain and suffering that humans are experiencing, and that is to go "in". Many people perhaps understand this concept, however, unless it is experienced, one can't truly recognise the nature of their own self and what it means. The senses and the thinking don't go where we exist and feel all life so it is a very hard task for me to explain and discuss the subject matter in this book.

When I came back to London, I looked for a teacher to help me through this, however, unfortunately, the spiritual industry can be more mind-boggling and corrupt than organised religion. I couldn't find anyone and one day I closed my eyes and fell into a deep meditative state for over an hour. That was the start of this journey. I listened to my body and observed my mind with extreme detail, which started a stream of totally new information about life. My family, my work, and my friends couldn't understand what was happening and how could I change so much and so many asked me to start compiling my thoughts and experiences in and out of meditations. Some warned about the dangers of an awakening and others asked me to keep going deeper. I now understand both of their perspectives.

Spiritual awakening is a very simple concept and can have levels of intensity. It can come upon through a "death" experience, plant medicine or via a teacher. This is simply when the mind recognises that there is something which it has overlooked. It sees the nature of our beings and hence the geometry and other psychedelic effects during a plant medicine experience, for example. In an awakening state, my brain realised that it was being controlled by Sebastian and that I was not him. Awakening leads to the separation of the being from mind and body.

Then the war started between me and him until the "thinking" Sebastian in my brain was eliminated, leading to me reclaiming control of my thoughts and emotions.

This war is between the "now" and "then". It is between "here" and there"; between my being and my conditioned thought.

It's a very painful and confusing war and hence, many people stop seeking upon having a spiritual experience and come to believe that they are free and liberated. This can lead to confusion, mental health issues and above all develop a toxic spiritual ego where they start believing that their thinking is god's thinking. The guidance, or paths, from an awakening state to a state of liberation, have been diluted and re-written over thousands of years of religious and yogic traditions. Now we humans have started following them blindly without context or a teacher.

The aim is to have no separation of thought and being in the now as that is where life happens, and hence have full control of and observation of one's own thoughts and actions.

In today's world, the casual use of plant medicine is leading to many events of spiritual awakenings all over the world. This, however, creates a bigger problem for the person, as they will always be in a whirlpool of the mind and society unless they work towards a) removing the thinker via introspective meditation, b) re-training the body and mind to be intelligent and free from the thinker and c) embodying stillness.

Plant medicines, like Ayahuasca, Mushrooms and DMT, are amazing tools for us to realise what we are: Stillness. This happens by the perceived speeding up of thinking, which could be attributed to the impact of these substances on neural pathways. For example, substances like psilocybin or DMT interact with serotonin receptors in the brain, leading to changes in perception and thought. As the speed of the movement of thought increases due to the heightened neurotransmission, there is a sense of awareness of the one that observes this change. When the change happens faster than usual, there is a realisation of the stillness against it. That is simply how these medicines facilitate an awakening. It's the speed of movement, against our very still nature.

These medicines can be life-changing, however, they need to be taken with caution, care and guidance on how to achieve and cultivate this stillness during and after the experience. There are many frameworks of self-realisation, most of them, however, are obsolete for the modern human. These include religions and yogic philosophies and within them, one can find different modalities and techniques on how to achieve every step in life towards claiming back your mind to the moment of now. Hence religions are called: "The way of life"

Today, these specific techniques, or modalities, which some people prefer over others, have become sects and branches of the main philosophies. Christian mysticism, Sufism, Theravada Buddhism, Sunni Islam, Jewish Mysticism and so on.

Most people follow a sect and their practices without understanding the context of the path and the larger philosophy behind it. We haven't been able to free our minds and bodies from the shackles of the conditioned thinker, and we remain a slave to our own thinking and age-old ways of achieving this peace.

By cultivating this stillness, one can eliminate the thinker and reclaim their mind and body, for the experience of life in the now, and hence be in union and sync with one's true being. This is what "Yoga" means: Union; and it has many names in other philosophies. Wahadat-al-Wajood in Islam, union with Christ in Christianity and so on.

During meditations, my brain reflected on my whole life to

realise that, like everyone else's, my life was designed by the data and information which was fed into the mind, and the quality of calories consumed by the body.

We are made to believe that we are our minds and bodies and that life, or your consciousness, is a result of mental activity, which is wrong both in the scientific and human world. It is not the ultimate truth and just the perspective of a very materialist (form and perception-based) thought framework which was laid down into Western philosophy during the time of René Descartes in 1600 when he said "I think, therefore I am".

For centuries before modern philosophy became a norm, humans believed in an aspect of life beyond perception. This was particularly strong in the cradle of civilisation, The Indus Valley, hence it thrived on peace and harmony for thousands of years.

I was asked by friends and family to write a story about how we came to believe that we are this limited and conditioned person, how that person then grows up and has dreams, desires and goals. I tell a story, questioning all that we humans experience growing up.

In this story, I write about my childhood, how I migrated to the UK and eventually became a very successful and known hospitality and entertainment entrepreneur. I cover my early days, my teenage sexual abuse, 9/11 and the constant struggle of trying to understand all these rules humans made for themselves. The story then moves on to my adult life.

I started my career as a journalist for the Wall Street Journal in London and eventually ended up trading financial instruments at various banks. In 2012, I left that world and started my own business to eventually bring innovation to the world of hospitality by creating a whole new industry called "Immersive Hospitality".

The world's first naked restaurant was my idea and creation - a subject which got press coverage in virtually every country in the world. Since then, other concepts I have designed have successfully run in London and abroad. I have been called a "maestro" by Forbes in my field and won multiple awards including recently the "Most Influential and Innovative Entertainment CEO"

These achievements however don't matter at all to me now. All of this is set up to strengthen the "I" and consequently lead to the creation of "another" and hence all the problems in the world.

Even when success came, I was unhappy - unhappy because of my own creative brain's curse. The moment you create something, your mind wants something else, something better. This is the story of all of us. We think there is a point in life where happiness exists i.e. if I get this or that or do this or that, I will be happy. That is simply not possible as the mind is designed to act on the past data it has. If you have been to the moon, you are not going to stop there and will aim for Mars. What next then? How far will we go in an ever-expanding minefield of consciousness and universe? The only way to understand reality and yourself is to look inside and understand the little "piece" of life and reality which is within us. Not physically within, but it is what we are made of.

Realise that we are not our bodies or our minds. Realise that we are not who we think we are. Realise that life here and its decisions are purely the brain's decisions. Realise that the brain makes these decisions autonomously, based on past data and experiences it gathers. Realise that all decisions are made in the now. Realise that thinking about those beforehand is useless. As much as the above is fascinating and interesting to hear, realise the true magic that your true existence is outside of this mental activity of the brain.

Only when we realise what we are, will we be full of life, love, joy and peace. Only by coming out of the brain, we can understand its limited nature and conditioning. Only by realising what you are, can you understand the workings of your own brain and the body and hence your life.

Over the course of writing this book, a whole new philosophy of experiencing life emerged. It was named Logical Humanism and the book was paused.

A few weeks following this extremely rare event, I left everything behind in London because my mind knew what it had to do now as it had knowledge of the true experiencer of life. Brexit, Covid, inflation and an acute cost of living crisis in the UK also prompted me to evaluate the business and the economics as it had become unprofitable in a matter of months. Nonetheless, leaving my home, work, relationships and life of 20 years in London was never going to be easy, especially as I had only a few hundred pounds left to spare. Everything else I had, was sold earlier and invested into the businesses.

During thousands of hours of deep meditation, practice and a self-sustained lifestyle in the mountains of Rhodes, Greece and Thailand, Logical Humanism continued to develop.

I ended up working with many people from all over the world and started helping them with their unrest. Meditation, movement, breathing and diet took top priority and a framework to achieve the Embodied Stillness or to embody the true self was created.

It is a framework of understanding and living the essence of life, purely from a place of one's own experience of being. It is the understanding that our true existence, where we feel and understand all life, sits outside of the phenomena of thinking and the computational power of the brain. The brain makes all its decisions, at a given moment, based on its conditioning, experience and data. Hence, all human decisions are coherent with the movement of life, which is cyclical and dual in nature, and out of our true being's direct control.

All experience of life is an internal phenomena and what you see is your perspective of reality. In order to change something or someone "out there" you have to change your perspective as the story of your life is only running in your mind, while you are observing it.

The experiencer of life, which is you, is in constant presence in knowing of life and this is not separate from what is being experienced.

In layman's terms, the experiencer is one, hence we can agree on the taste of mango and the smell of rose for example. Hence we feel the pain of others. We will discuss more about these concepts later.

In a world full of conflict and friction, where we try and change others, I believe that the ancient Eastern philosophies of understanding the internal world, need to marry with Western thinking to bring about a new understanding of how to live peacefully personally and socially.

Following the emergence of this philosophy (Logical Humanism), associated framework (Embodied Stillness) and modalities (ways and routines) to cultivate stillness and claim back our brain and bodies from social and conditioned thinking, I was asked by many to compile a short book which could help people enquire into the nature of the one experiencing life right now. This is that book.

The thesis on Logical Humanism is a larger, ongoing work which I will compile and share in due course, however in the last few months many people all over the world have adopted it as a way of understanding and living their own lives.

In this book, I write my realisations in and out of meditation and I hope they will make you question the nature of your own being.

I believe it is time to realise and live the truth so we can rid ourselves of all of this suffering that our minds create. It is time to realise the real you so a new paradigm of peace and stillness can prevail, within and without our bodies.

In no particular order, I present to you my realisations hoping you can connect with them and that they will help you to go deeper in investigating your true nature.

Sebastian Lyall

Realisations
&
Meditations

You are not this person you have to come to believe you are.

This person and their personality changes, however, the one which is aware of that change, doesn't change.

That is you.

WHAT ARE YOU?

You are not the change you observe.

You are the knowledge and knowing of that change.

WHAT ARE YOU?

Life changes, people change, personalities change and situations change.

But ask yourself, while everything has always been changing, have you really changed? The one experiencing all life. Has that changed?

The answer will be no.

Experiences change, the experiencer doesn't change.

WHAT ARE YOU?

You were here last night, a week ago, a month ago and on your 13th birthday.

Remember saying "my" 13th birthday or my graduation?

That "my" is always here.

All that is perception, and that we call life, is in a constant state of flux but the experiencer of it never changes with the change.

WHAT ARE YOU?

We think and are told that we evolving, growing and becoming better.

This is against our own experience of life.

We don't change.

The movie of life is changing.

And we are the stillness which is viewing this movie.

WHAT ARE YOU?

You are not the person you have come to believe you are.

You are the knowledge and understanding of the change in this person and their personality.

This person thinks perpetually based on all previous thoughts and experiences.

And you the knower and observer of this stream of thought.

WHAT ARE YOU?

All that is moving, all that is changing.

Inside you and outside you.

Is because of the stillness you are.

WHAT ARE YOU?

When you see someone in physical pain, you also feel the pain.

Have you ever wondered why?

You feel it simply because you feel it.

You are not separate from anyone.

Accept what you experience as your experience of life is the ultimate reality and not what has been programmed into you.

I ask myself and you should ask yourselves too, who is using your brain and body?

Am I in total control of my thought and action. Do my thoughts and actions arise from a place of my being?

Or is Sebastian thinking for me? And what is Sebastian? A bunch of old thoughts accumulated in a personality in my brain.

Is this person you think you are, using your brain?

WHAT ARE YOU?

Ask yourself, who is at unrest?

You or your brain?

Those are two different concepts.

WHAT ARE YOU?

Thoughts are a stream of information, which is constantly observed by us.

We have a name for this stream; life.

All that you see and observe in life is a continuous stream of thought.

This stream of thought is represented as time.

It's like sitting in a cafe in Paris and watching people pass by; you are not the movement of people you observe.

You are not your stream of thinking.

You are observing it, in stillness.

WHAT ARE YOU?

A thought is based on previous thoughts. And what is it?

What actually is a thought?

An energy flow in neural pathways where it has flown before. This creates thought, action and all experienced life.

It's an autonomous process and can't be changed from within as no new pathways demand energy from the food and oxygen you consume. Thus no new and original thought is created and all thoughts become perpetual and conditioned in nature.

Unless you come out of thought itself and observe it with total keenness.

That is meditation. That is metacognition.

We have learned what to do "with" the human body and mind.

We haven't, however, learned what to do "to" this body and mind.

We didn't learn or were taught, how to properly take care of these tools we use daily.

My brain had a memory of a personality, Sebastian, and it allowed this personality to use it.

What is this personality, Sebastian? An accumulation of thought and experience until a certain point in time. He then changes as his thoughts and actions change.

Thus, Sebastian changes every moment, but my knowing of him doesn't.

He changes, I don't.

WHAT ARE YOU?

The person you are looking for is already here, inside you. The one who only wants to be, express creativity and give love.

It was inside me all along.

It's just that Sebastian was using my brain and body.

I realised, that his thinking, including his desires and fears, were not mine.

WHAT ARE YOU?

Stillness is a state of being which exists outside of the stream of thought.

It's a place where you feel all life including the love for your pet, the taste of your food and the smell of roses.

This peaceful sense of a place is what you call "I am" and it is within you too, resting and waiting to be claimed by you.

You can call it your soul, but it is indeed just you.

WHAT ARE YOU?

A movement can't experience another movement.

Stillness is needed to observe any movement effectively, hence we need to embody our still nature to observe the movement of life effectively.

That stillness is what you are. It's in you and around you. It's what you are made of.

This stillness feels like love and harmony, and that is what it means when you hear people preach "we are love".

Observe nature and you will observe that all movement happens against the extreme stillness of your knowing.

Knowing of all movement.

WHAT ARE YOU?

There is no difference between anyone's life experience.

Rose smells the same to everyone.

The difference is in perception and preferences.

WHAT ARE YOU?

Step out of the movement to analyse it and potentially change it.

Thought is a movement as well and it can't be analysed from within.

Meditation and listening are the only ways to create neuroplasticity and change in the brain.

If you were given a fruit you never tasted before, the moment you taste it you will "know" and recognise its flavour. For example the knowledge of the taste of mango.

Tasting is a first-hand experience that no one teaches you.

Ask yourself, how do you know the taste? How do you recognise the taste the first time you taste anything?

Because you just know. You know it already and information is essentially meeting its source.

Not just a fruit or mango. But all life. You know it because you are the source of all information and the destination of it too.

All life experiences are already within you.

WHAT ARE YOU?

How do you and I agree on the smell of sage or the taste of coffee or, for that matter, on any life experience?

We agree and recognise because the experiencer, or what you call "I am", is the same.

Our brains and bodies are different nodes sending all experiences to a single source.

That is why you feel the satisfaction when you feed someone.

WHAT ARE YOU?

The nature of experiences is very different from the nature of the experiencer.

Dive into the world of the experiencer and you will find peace, harmony and love.

Nothing is really hard or easy. These are subjective definitions in our brains.

Climbing a mountain is only hard because you think it's hard. Ask a mountaineer and they have a different idea about it.

A mountain is not even high. It's higher, relative to some places. Ask the people who live in the mountains, and for them, the mountains aren't high.

A mountain becomes high and difficult to climb because we think it is. And who told us this when we were kids?

WHAT ARE YOU?

Realise that life and its decisions are the brain's decisions.

Realise that the brain makes its decisions autonomously based on experience and data it has gathered in the past.

Realise that all decisions are made in the now and are perfectly coherent with the movement of life, as the brain uses all the information it has, at that time, to make these decisions.

As all decisions are made in the now, no need to think about them beforehand.

As much as this is magic, realise the true magic of your existence, which is outside of this movement of the brain.

We always want to become like someone; a better version of ourselves perhaps.

This is against the very nature of our being and experience of life, hence we keep chasing this better version.

We don't change. Experience and life changes.

We don't evolve. We just experience evolution and change.

WHAT ARE YOU?

Ask yourself, is there another version of yourself in your brain right now, who you aspire to?

The answer most likely is yes.

What is this version made up of? Or are there many versions? Perhaps one which your family wants and the other which your work requires.

Our brains are used by all these personalities we want to become. The solution is to understand in reality there is no personality to start with.

There was never a Sebastian, as he was a different idea in different people's minds.

The better version of you, which is in your mind and the one you want to be like every moment of life; that person is an illusion and not real.

That person is an amalgamation of all the "good" in the world. They are invincible and can't possibly exist.

When your brains defined this "good" with language, based on your background and limited experiences, "bad" also came into being.

Bad is also made by you. It is also made of you. This bad isn't bad for a lot of people out there either, it's just bad for you.

This "good" person, version 2.0 of yourself, is an unachievable aim that culture, language and history have planted in our brains.

Liberate yourself from this programming as doesn't serve any purpose.

Health and peace can only be truly achieved when one realises their true nature and returns to it.

The end of seeking and suffering can only be realised when you embody your true still nature, outside of the thinking brain.

All external experiences are created and consumed via someone's thoughts and perceptions.

The only true and unique experience is the experience of living.

And that is internal, not external.

That is the only experience we came here for.

WHAT ARE YOU?

Life is a constant movement of thoughts.

A movement which can be observed and understood.

Peace comes only when you realise that you are not in this movement, but you exist in stillness observing it.

WHAT ARE YOU?

To understand and appreciate a movement, one has to be very still.

A movement can't be observed if you are in the movement.

Life will feel out of sync if you think you are this thinking and changing person.

You live in the now. All your life experiences happen in the now. You have never been to "then" and as soon as you are there, it is indeed now.

Time, my friends, is the difference between now and then.

For our being and experience of life, there is no concept of time as we stay in the now. Always.

The brain, yes, has a container of time and space to keep our memories so we know how to eat, drink and be safe.

It's as if this container is in your head, in sort of a unidirectional rectangular shape, which allows memories about the past and plans about the future to be stored. However, if you observe closely, you will realise your life is always in the now part of that container and that your experience of life always happens in the current moment.

And in this container, there lives a thinker. The person you think you are and who is thinking for you right now.

When I realised that, I understood I was very different from what Sebastian had become in that container.

WHAT ARE YOU?

The beauty, or curse, you see is not out there. It's in here. In you.

All that is experienced is happening inside you; in your body and in your mind.

A whole universe resides in but it looks as if it's outside.

That is the uncomfortable truth.

Ask yourself, in your world, is the thinker of your life's decisions different from the one experiencing it?

Is the thinker in your brain different from you?

WHAT ARE YOU?

The mind will never understand the nature of our beings. The mind is programmed to think about things, desires, problems and work.

It is programmed to look out and do.

The challenge is how does it know that it is programmed. Can it? Unfortunately, it is programmed not to know.

Unless, you observe your thoughts and actions with absolute focus and clarity, in the absence of the compulsions of the brain. In the absence of this person, you think you are.

This can only happen in deep meditation or love.

WHAT ARE YOU?

To create change, all you really have to do is observe the thought of now.

That is where change starts.

But it's very hard as we don't have access to our brains.

It's being used by this person you think you are.

That person exists far away from the "now".

Your brain needs new, fresh data to create change. But the brain works on previous thoughts. That is the nature of it.

So how does one bring up true change?

One has to change the source of thought from perception and outward knowledge, which is conditioned in nature, to the eternal knowledge of our existence.

The brain needs to change the source to you from the person you think you are.

It's you against yourself.

Thoughts lead to actions and actions matter.

Yes.

But actions only happen in the now. So clearly, only the thought of now matters.

Only entertain the thought of now and park all other thoughts in your brain.

When the time comes, actions based on those thoughts shall be made if necessary.

WHAT ARE YOU?

All your worldly desires have been programmed into your brain.

In reality, they have nothing to do with you as they are not yours.

Ask yourself, what is it really that you desire?

The answer will be health and love.

WHAT ARE YOU?

All our mind's desires have a root in our past.

It's data injection and programming which was done to your brain, and all human desires stem from there.

Following a desire, beyond the desire to exist, means following your past patterned behaviour.

Accept all thoughts of desires but don't follow them. Just focus on what you need to do now.

When and if the time is right, these desires may be fulfilled.

If a desire arises, let it.

Don't entertain and act on it compulsively.

If it's a true desire, your actions will naturally change over the course of life to achieve that.

If it's not your true desire, it will evaporate in your mind's ether

WHAT ARE YOU?

A desire is a thought which translates into "you are not happy now".

Ask yourself, why would you entertain any thought which takes you away from now?

Now is the only time you have.

WHAT ARE YOU?

Thoughts, desires, plans and fears are an autonomous movement, based on past thoughts.

Thoughts come and go if allowed to, and you are the observation of them.

You don't move with them. That is against your nature.

Observe them in meditation and let them continue their natural flow.

Knowledge in thoughts can only be realised when they move and you remain still.

You carry many different wannabe personalities in your mind who are using your mind.

You are the only one and you know what you are.

Ask yourself and you will realise you are being, which is full of just love and compassion

WHAT ARE YOU?

Every thought is great.

Every thought has a whole universe hidden in it, only if observed.

All life happens inside you. What looks outside is happening inside you as your perspective.

That is why self-care is needed. Not cosmetic, but deep internal care of body and mind.

If you feel good, you have better thoughts, which lead to better action and hence better physical reality.

Not just for you, but for many!

Everything everywhere is starting now and here.

Just that Sebastian doesn't believe it and for him, "there" and "then" exist.

For me and you however it's different as we never went to "there" or "then".

It's always here and now for us.

WHAT ARE YOU?

We look for peace and stillness all our lives. The stillness which is within us.

We just seek experiences which enable us to realise that. It is always here waiting for us to be realised.

Sunsets, love, holidays and family - everything we seek is to give us that feeling of pausing of time.

That is when you embody your true nature.

WHAT ARE YOU?

The childlike sense of living is hidden deep within us.

Investigate the nature of your inner being to reignite that sense.

It's a special sense that you hold and it's only yours.

WHAT ARE YOU?

When was the last time you took time to pause and take proper care of yourself?

All your life experiences correlate with your inner well-being.

Remind yourself that every day.

We worry about money all the time. Even when there is no need to worry.

If you have a penny more than you need right now, you are fine. Do you? I assume you do.

And right now? And now? And...

And this is life. In the now.

This now creates a reality which we observe and call the universe.

Unhappiness in relationships is useless. Excessive thinking about one's partner doesn't lead you anywhere.

Step back from the drama of thought and conversation to realise that your partner is exactly the person you desire.

With that comes all of their personality, not just what you consider "good".

It's impossible for them to be "good" for you all the time.

It's not how reality and life works.

WHAT ARE YOU?

The fear of death is one of the biggest hindrances for humans to be fearless and loving.

This fear comes from a) not understanding the nature of our beings and b) subscribing to the "thinkers" idea of time.

Our body and mind will die, but the knower of life lives and exists in a formless and eternal state.

That knower of life is what you mean when you say "I am".

That never dies.

WHAT ARE YOU?

Everyone carries a whole universe in their brains, of which you as a person have limited to no knowledge.

Realising that will bring out your true nature of love for everyone and everything.

No one is poor really. Their situation is poor, yes, and that can change.

How? Well, first you have to believe that you are not poor so your thinking and action are not poor.

If you think you're poor, then your thinking is rooted in the conditioned definition of what you call "poor". How will change ever come?

Real change comes when you realise what you are, against the movement of thought and thinking,

It comes when you inject new data into the brain via meditation and observation of your own thoughts and actions.

WHAT ARE YOU?

Know your body. Understand your brain. Look and feel them from an objective point of view.

Learn from the knowledge in the movement of thought and sensation. What do you see when you observe all thoughts and sensations?

Observe them in meditation. All thoughts. All sensations. All feelings. As they pass by.

Don't judge, just observe.

Then you will understand what is going on inside you, so you can make use of your body and mind properly to create the reality in which love and happiness can prevail.

The brain's function is to protect you and be there for you so you can function and live properly. Express and show love and show your very nature.

Sadly it's been stolen by society, by social and culturally driven addictions.

It has been stolen by this person you think you are.

Mine was stolen by Sebastian and his thinking.

It's time to realise and ask this question, who is thinking for you?

WHAT ARE YOU?

Watch your own actions. Watch your own movement.

Your body and mind are performing many actions autonomously.

Driving. Cooking. Cleaning. Walking.

Observe yourself and slowly you can realise that you are the stillness which is the knowing of all life's movement.

Your experience of life depends on the movement of life within you.

Life is all that is happening within you, and without it, you won't be alive.

For this movement to happen naturally, one has to embody stillness.

Once the internal systems start moving, your external reality also starts changing through thought and action.

WHAT ARE YOU?

To experience anything with any expectation of an outcome is to experience it with someone else eyes.

For an authentic and personal experience, remove expectations and just observe.

Listen.

If there is a listener, there is change.

The listener can be anyone. Including yourself.

So listen to yourself.

WHAT ARE YOU?

The moment you observe your fears or worries. The moment you actually look at them in meditation.

They dissolve.

The moment you allow the movement of thought, everything evaporates and only the knowing of it all remains.

Only you will remain.

There is a self-organising structure at every level of existence.

The atoms, the molecules, the cells, humans, societies, cities, counties, planets, solar systems, galaxies... all have a structure which dictates consciousness above the level of observation.

For humans, the knowing of life is a level above the movement of our body and brain.

By training the structure and movement of life inside us (cellular and nervous systems), we can let them do the work for us.

So we can rest and be in our natural state of stillness.

Accept and listen to all offerings.

Don't resist.

Don't let your mind, and this person you think you are, not do things which can improve your health and outlook on life.

Listen to everything without the noise of your own perspective and thoughts. Without right or wrong.

There are opportunities for physical and mental transformation in every word listened.

The love you have for your parents will never change. The love they have for you never changes either.

Personalities change and hence expressions may change and all of this is due to new circumstances and memory of how to deal with these unknown situations.

It is simply a series of events which can change a person.

So I ask myself and you should too; has the love changed between you and your parents or has the perception of that love changed?

The love which exists beyond expression and perception is the only true love.

Look into their eyes in silence next time and you will find the answer.

WHAT ARE YOU?

Try eating only when you are absolutely hungry. Food is fuel and medicine for your body and we should learn to treat it as such.

This means if you think about what to eat, or are led by habit, you aren't hungry.

Real hunger will move your body to acquire food automatically. There is no thought when this happens.

That is when we should only be eating and not because it's a certain time in the day.

Everything which you don't need has a memory attached to it. Everything, subconsciously, engages neural pathways in the brain which demand energy.

By decluttering our spaces, we can clean our minds and reclaim a big part of our brain power.

Fill your homes with natural products and healthy whole foods instead to restrict chemicals which may be harming your gut and skin.

When eating, only eat and try and follow the flavours with every bite.

Sitting straight and closing your eyes for the first few bites will help remind you of the difference between the chewer and the taster of food.

Immerse in the experience every time you eat.

Take a few moments to sit by the bed when waking up and, with your eyes closed, feel your body from your toes to your head.

Be aware of your body and move it slowly before it is going to do a hard day's work.

Using meditative music will help you to stay calm and still as you start the day.

WHAT ARE YOU?

Try sitting with the back straight as much as you can.
If you sit on the base of your thighs, not on your bum, you
will see the back will become erect.

If it's not comfortable, your body will tell you which part
needs work.

Listen to it. Don't let your life story ignore these messages.

WHAT ARE YOU?

Bathing with love to observe the movement of water on our bodies helps us to realise stillness.

Washing our faces while touching sensors behind and in our ears can help in proprioceptive feedback of the body's position in time and space.

Cleaning our sinuses several times a day, allows the most important aspect of life to continue naturally: breathing.

Observe yourself doing all this and know that you are stillness which knows all this movement.

Move as much as you can.

Stretch as much as you can.

The movement will allow you to achieve both inner and outer health.

WHAT ARE YOU?

Learn how to breathe properly and you can fix a lot of issues with your health.

Most of us don't know how to breathe and we still expect our bodies to work perfectly. We were never taught to breathe or we never bothered listening.

Inhale from the nose and push your stomach out as air enters your body. You should feel only your naval area expanding.

Exhale from the mouth and contract your pelvic area and stomach.

Exhale when making any moves while exercising and doing daily chores. Inhale at rest or in a passive pose.

Train your body to naturally allow this movement to happen.

Experience life in the now and you will be able to analyse the whole flow of it.

You will understand the evolution of it.

That is the only way one can make sense of it.

Only the thought of now serves your true purpose.
The rest is just a story, which never stops, and it only takes
you away from the now.

Every moment, know of everything but only do of the now.

True love can only be realised between two people when there is no "I" in either person.

Love is not what a person does to another. Love is all there is, behind our personalities and preferences.

Try and spend a few hours silent with your loved ones.

You will have more conversations than when you actually talk.

Excessive talking is just different perceptions fighting for the top spot.

WHAT ARE YOU?

The love you want is already around you. Listen to what your friends and family are saying about you.

They love you. They thank you.

Accept it.

Understand that they can see what you can't.

One's judgment about oneself is often clouded by not accepting love and gratitude.

Even when someone loves us from the bottom of their hearts, our minds make up another personality who doesn't want to accept this.

That is not you.

We all want to change someone, but where is this desire coming from?

Is it coming from you wanting a healthy and good relationship with them? That doesn't sound bad, does it?

Or is it you that you want them to be happy as they are?

The former is friction as there is an "I" that desires, even if the desire is considered good.

The other is love.

There is a difference between rejecting everyone's opinions, which most of us do when we go on a spiritual journey, and rejecting one's own opinions.

Spirituality, philosophies and religions aim to help in the understanding that the problem is our own opinions, not someone else's.

It only can be possible when you realise what is the source of your opinions.

And for that, you have to look hard.

I realised that I didn't come here to entertain the desires of Sebastian.

But I realised only after I found out that Sebastian was not me but an amalgamation of thought, action and experience.

A social and cultural "personality" sitting in my mind, dictating all my thoughts, actions and hence reality.

We don't accumulate anything. We just observe the personality and its thoughts in the now.

WHAT ARE YOU?

When your life moves very fast and some unexpected events come up, good or bad, ask yourself if the knower of everything that changed in life has also changed.

Or are you the unchanging and still while life changes?

WHAT ARE YOU?

Ask yourself, don't you already know how life should be spent?

Don't you already have all the knowledge needed to live a good life?

Is your deeper inner opinion correct because it stems from a place of love?

The answer will be yes.

The brain however is different.

So watch when you speak and analyse the source of this speech.

Is it the brain and its conditioning or the truth of love?

Never assume you have all the answers, as the answers are in one's mind.

The reality is in observation only. Not in the thinking and the doing.

Experiencing life is the knowledge of your senses for yourself.

Expressing life is the doing of good for others.

The first is what we experience, and the latter is what our minds and bodies do to generate that experience.

WHAT ARE YOU?

A desire creates an expectation for tomorrow.

An expectation of a specific outcome tomorrow.

But the fear of failure is created today.

And we don't live in tomorrow.

But because of our desires, we do live a life in fear.

WHAT ARE YOU?

If you desire to be always right in front of friends and family, you are in the wrong to start with.

Truth doesn't need any validation.

This desire to be right is that of the brain's, not yours

It's not your fear. It's just a fear.

Look at it and see why you are experiencing it.

Just observe the reasoning behind it and you will realise, it's not the fear itself but what you "think" may happen.

But has it happened? No.

However, if you think it may happen, then it will.

It's simple really.

Thoughts are generated continuously by other thoughts.
It's a stream of history, perpetually connected.

Ask yourself, do you want to entertain this burden of
history?

By entertaining any thoughts, desires or emotions, you are
entertaining your burden.

Even if the burden is a day old.

WHAT ARE YOU?

My body was moved by Sebastian for years until I realised that he lives in the past and future and thus has little idea of my needs.

So ask yourself who is moving your body?

You or the thinker in your brain?

WHAT ARE YOU?

Whatever you feel is totally happening inside of you. If you heard something you didn't like or you don't appreciate someone's attitude towards you, look in and ask yourself this.

"Why is it that I feel this way?"

You will find answers in your past experiences.

WHAT ARE YOU?

What you hear and feel is what your brain wants to hear and feel.

The emotional response to any event or conversation is not an external phenomenon.

It's not the other who triggers you. It's your own past and programming which triggers you.

All your fears are rooted in worry of a desire that may not be fulfilled.

Follow that desire to see where it is coming from.

Is it truly yours?

WHAT ARE YOU?

Your dad has an image of you. Your mum has another.
Your partner and your friends have another.

And you have an image of yourself.

So ask yourself, which one are you?

Which is the reality?

The answer is outside of these images.

WHAT ARE YOU?

Most of our frustrations don't stem from the subject of frustration itself, but from the fact that we can't act on it.

And the inability to act is rooted in our past experiences.

Observe why you can't talk or do something which, in that moment could be simply done, and you will find the answer in your life history.

WHAT ARE YOU?

Ask yourself, would you rather live a life of a perspective which is limited to your past, or drop that perspective to adopt the universal perspective which rests on respect for life?

Teach someone how to love and even though your body will die at some point, you will live for eternity.

If you want to change something in someone, ask yourself first why you want that change.

You will realise that it's actually something you want to change in yourself.

Simply because what you experience is your perspective of reality, not the ultimate reality.

To change someone, you have to change yourself and your perspective.

The easiest way? Drop all your perspective and just accept and give love.

WHAT ARE YOU?

Experience and knowing of life happens in the nothingness between the stories of life each of our minds plays out.

WHAT ARE YOU?

Your only job is to seek the nature of your being. Your only question should be "What is that, which experiences the taste of coffee or the love for one's parents?"

Your job and role in this world will be revealed to you in the process of this self-discovery.

The human mind may be evil to each other at times. Many times.

Human nature however is never evil.

It's just that we have forgotten which one are we.

WHAT ARE YOU?

Happiness comes not because of the experience itself, but realised due to the health of the experiencer.

A piece of bread (actually all life experiences) will taste better for someone who is healthy, regardless of their wealth and status in society.

The quality of one's life experience doesn't depend on the kind of experience but on the inner workings of the human body and mind.

As a personality, you are nothing but an illusion, simply because everyone, including yourself, has a different idea of you in their head. So there isn't a single personality.

However, as the experiencer of life, you are everything, everywhere.

Seek the nature of the experiencer of life and you shall get all the answers.

WHAT ARE YOU?

Happiness comes not when you have a knowledgeable perspective, but is realised when you drop all your mind's conditioned perspectives and only observe what's happening to you, and around you.

That is the only way to adapt all possible perspectives, hence nudging you closer to the absolute truth.

Imagine watching a movie where you put on a new set of glasses and everything looks pretty and amazing.

In the movie of life, these good glasses are called "one's mindset", which is in your control. To change it, however, you have to come out of it. Totally and completely.

You have to meditate and be still so that the mind looks inside in introspection and creates this change by understanding the nature of reality.

Essentially, by understanding you and your being.

Listen to everyone and everything. Accept keenly what is being said and advised.

Meanwhile, continue doing what you have to do in the now.

Continue connecting with your life in the now.

If the advice a worthwhile, when the time comes, it is sure to become a reality.

If you feel out of love, look at your mind and analyse what is it doing. Is it in sync with you, the experiencer of life?

Or is it planning and thinking hence keeping you away from love?

You will find something you may be doing which made you feel "out" of love.

Being in love is our natural state.

Your mind will give you everything from tips, techniques, excitement, medicine, work, tricks and hope to keep you entertained and mask the fact that it has the power to keep you away from the only thing you really want.

Stillness in love.

Money comes when clarity comes.
Clarity comes when money isn't in your thoughts.

WHAT ARE YOU?

You think you have a personality, but that personality is only in your mind.

It's limited to your knowledge and no one else knows about it really. It's an assumed personality of yourself, which creates conflict with others and hence keeps you away from all the love you are supposed to receive.

Drop the whole personality, the "I" or "Mine", to understand that your self, which experiences life, isn't some petty assumed personality.

It's much bigger and beyond this personality and its thoughts.

All humans really desire is to have an original thought. Their own understanding of life and reality.

Ask yourself this, how can this come from your own conditioned and programmed stream of thoughts?

It comes in observation of all thought. It comes in meditation.

WHAT ARE YOU?

Ask yourself, do you want to just experience a shared reality which has been programmed into you, or do you want to experience reality in its totality?

A tree is defined as such but, without a definition, it's a totally new being to be observed.

Without your personality's limited perspective and definitions, you can see everything in the way that everything should be seen.

With love. With awe. With stillness.

WHAT ARE YOU?

The experience of life, which is your only experience, is actually happening when you are waiting for life to happen.

You are living in your own matrix, if you have any expectations of something which may happen.

Do what you have to do right now. Don't remove focus from that. If it's eating, just eat. If it's having tea, then just do that. If closing the eyes helps, do that but be immersed.

And tell all other thoughts.

"Hang on a second. I will give you plenty of my time and attention in meditation"

Living with the thought of now and meditating on all other thoughts is the natural flow of life.

It's only when you embody stillness that your body realises it needs to move to let you be yourself.

This human body then becomes active to create this stillness and the experience of life becomes healthy and joyful.

This stillness is the place around which all movement happens. It allows the movement to happen within and with-out the body.

Cultivating this stillness in exercises, breathing, eating, bathing and any other daily activities will make your life experience more alert, aware, active and adoring.

Conversations in relationships, especially when done over technology, are bound to be two perspectives shouting at each other.

There is hardly any listening from either side.

You have to be grounded deeply in love to be able to cope with friction arising from opposing thoughts and perceptions in conversations.

You have to be still and understand the programming behind the conversation so it passes and you remain in a place of love.

Doing right now, what you desire to do at some point in life, will bring you joy and perhaps even money.

Doing anything only for money will certainly bring suffering and confusion.

WHAT ARE YOU?

All life happens in the now. The moment in which you are reading this.

If you want to share any aspect of life with someone, this is the only time.

Now.

Experience of life is very different from the story of life.

Don't just live in a story but make your own story.

In love you become still not because something stops around you, but because you only experience life and not the drama of thought.

You become a pure life experience as you drop this personality and its thinking.

Only in the presence of love, does one realise what it means to live and experience the now, without the distractions of the personality in the brain.

Only in love, we can be ourselves.

WHAT ARE YOU?

When we converse with a loved one, if we don't drop our personality and the thoughts associated with it, then have we even conversed?

If we stay in our minds, we don't listen and we miss the love for which we wanted to converse in the first place.

WHAT ARE YOU?

How many times you have thought "I don't have time for myself?"

Ask yourself, what do you have time for then because clearly time is passing and you must be doing something.

Challenge your mind's habits and the cycle you are stuck in.

It's indeed incredibly hard to break it. At least observe it and know that, it is this person you think you are, who is stopping you from getting better and happy.

Realise you are not this person and train your brain via embodying stillness.

Ambition, individuality and desires create a very strong sense of "I".

This "I" will take you away from love and hence your true self.

This true self is what you really are.

The experiencer of life, that does everything for love.

Your past is a memory in your brain. It is part of your brain. You can dilute it but it will never leave you.

However, you can certainly leave it by realising that your life experience is just this moment and every moment spent becomes the past.

Spend it in love and this moment can stay with you forever.

The only way to experience true love is to stop wanting and thinking about it.

Only when all of your personality's desires, including the desire to love are ignored, you will be able to accept all the love you are here to receive.

The realisation of your true self is not an experience for an individual.

It's the abolishment of the individual experience.

WHAT ARE YOU?

If one feels sad or frustrated, it is a reflection of the inner struggle one has.

It is because of something you are doing that you know isn't right. It could be basic things such as buying excessive plastic or eating unhealthy food.

There is a continuous friction between what is and what you think should be. And this loop is non-stop.

There can never be a problem out there, as your life experience is just a story running in your mind,

Your life is just your perspective, not good or bad, but just yours.

To make yourself happy, you have to change your perspective and nothing else.

Unless we understand this nature of reality, we are all living in thought and opinions, and there you will find pain, war, suffering and struggle.

If you observe keenly, you will realise that the experiencer
of life is different from the one acting it out.

One is living life and one is thinking about it,

Iur life aim is to sync them in unity.

WHAT ARE YOU?

Investigate the nature of your being, the one which experiences all life, and you may realise, with practice and patience, that the experiencer is one and it is everywhere.

Hence the divisions between the experience and the experiencer are an illusion.

In actuality, you are experiencing yourself when you experience life.

WHAT ARE YOU?

All outward knowledge is limited to someone else's experience of life.

It is limited to their knowledge, life and perception of the world.

You are essentially listening to someone else's mind.

Sure, always listen, but why don't you let your mind also listen to you?

After all, you know life and all its experiences exactly the same way as anyone else.

This is only possible in meditation. Out of meditation, we are engaged with the mind and it's programming without even realising that.

If you observe closely, you can find yourself in every movement you observe.

Simply because your knowledge of life is the stillness which is enabling all movement.

You are enabling all life.

WHAT ARE YOU?

Our idea of reality is limited to our background and conditioning. Not only that, human perception is limited to five senses.

However, that is just the brain and body. Not you.

You are much bigger than this. You are the source of all perceptive reality. It starts with you and ends with you.

WHAT ARE YOU?

There is no difference in anything in reality.

It just looks different in the reality we observe, and that is also fascinating.

WHAT ARE YOU?

Everything is a movement.

Everything passes.

Everything changes.

Let it be.

Only you stay still.

Only you are the unchanging.

WHAT ARE YOU?

Humans are transformed by their own watch and not by their their own thought.

Watching your thoughts and actions is an incredibly hard task but it is the only way true change happens.

Meditation is reclaiming your life from society and its conditioned way.

It is also reclaiming your life from this person you think you are, which represents all that society is.

Once you embody stillness, you can truly be yourself.

Meditation is a strive to be and know yourself.

A mind will only follow a specific and conditioned path unless acted upon by an outside force.

If you get a chance to meet any such force, consider yourself lucky.

To experience anything with an expectation is to have someone else's recycled experience.

Your expectation is linked to something you were told at some point by someone.

"Life is this way, but should be that way," they said.

Magic only happens when you let life experiences show their true nature to you, without any expectations.

WHAT ARE YOU?

By only choosing to do the things you have a strong liking for, you end up experiencing a minuscule part of reality and existence.

Open up to all experiences being offered to you.

Open up to life.

You can have everything you want, Literary, everything.

Only that the price of everything is everything.

To have everything you have to give up everything; not what you own but what you think.

All definitions of what is good and what is bad.

When you remove all conditioned concepts from the mind, you end up living the essence of life and existence.

That is truly when you have everything.

WHAT ARE YOU?

The experience of life is dualistic in nature. Day leads to night and night to day. Peace to war and war to peace. Pain to health and so on.

One can't exist without the other. It is the Yin Yang and Circle of Life, we all talk about.

Think about it, will you even know what darkness is if there were no light?

This is this stream of duality which we are here to experience. You came here to experience all the life of this person you think you are. Not just the good, but all of it.

I came to experience Sebastian's life in its totality.

WHAT ARE YOU?

There is no right or wrong. No good or bad. There just "is".

All minds are doing what they can do based on all the information they have. We are lost in the drama of thought and perception to forget that life happens at a very different level.

One has to remove all the mind's preferences, all likes and dislikes; it has to drop its perspective totally for it to have the brain power to see the beauty of what is.

The human brain is programmed to be very proud of the culture and traditions it has experienced, forgetting that these are just habits of certain people influenced by climate, food and laws.

This is nothing sacred or special and should be viewed as such.

What is sacred is life and love, and that we destroy in the name of culture and identity.

WHAT ARE YOU?

All religions and philosophies are simply ways for people of different cultures to achieve peace and happiness. To embody stillness and hence become god's eye to their own thoughts and actions. That is the message and hallmark of many religions and philosophies.

What we have forgotten is that these ways have been diluted and taken out of context over years of stories.

Ask yourself, what was your prophet or teacher doing when they became a good person? When they found god?

Meditating.

And who were they talking to in meditation? They were observing their own minds with objectivity. In that, they got the knowledge of what actually life is and how shared happiness can be achieved.

To make it easier, we humans created a concept and named this shared happiness God, Allah, Krishna, Shiva and other deities

Follow whichever philosophy you want in an attempt to achieve this stillness and observation of your own actions. But do it with a clear understanding and context.

WHAT ARE YOU?

Liberate yourself from your own thoughts by understanding that all you have to do is to decide on what you are doing now.

If you are cooking, all decision-making has to be about the act of cooking and nothing else. If sitting and having tea, it has to be about the taste and what are you going to look at.

The rest will take care of itself when it enters the now.

All choices are made by the brain in the now.

If someone asked me "tea or coffee?" there would be an instant decision.

That decision is the brain's decision based on its preferences and past knowledge.

The next thought is that Sebastian, the personality, made a decision. It tries to own it, however, the decision is purely autonomous and is based on the past.

Free yourself from excessive thinking by realising that all choices and decisions are made in the now, by the brain, and it does it with all the knowledge it has.

It will make the right decision when the time comes for it. That is its only job.

How can you experience your true nature?

Simply, by being still and observing all other
expressions of life.

By listening to what's happening in and around you

Ask yourself, do you want to spend the time on living life or, waste it by thinking about spending life in the future?

Time is the only thing you have here on earth.

Meditation is the medicine for humans to fix society.

We humans are hurting.

Not because of what is happening in the world but because of the conflict in our own brains.

On one side, we just want to be and feel all that is love and on the other side, we want things and experiences that take us away from the same love and a sense of being still.

The nature of reality is simply this; if you are hurting it is not because of an experience. It is because of your definition of that experience, as clearly how can any experience in this world be bad? And didn't we say bad exists because we defined the good?

This internal struggle between the thinker and ourselves is then projected out in our relationships as breakups and on a global level as atrocities, poverty and war.

The human mind is designed to consume more. This want is not limited to things and experiences but also extreme ambition and the desire for personal growth.

In pursuit of all of what has been programmed in our minds, we forget to live life and time flies. It is simply because time is represented as a stream of thought and the more thought you have about all that you want, the faster life passes by. We all know that in love and peace, this phenomenon reverses and time slows down. We sometimes even feel that time stops. This is the moment when we achieve our true nature of stillness as the story of life in our brains slows down.

It is time for us to understand that the nature of reality is very different from what we have been taught and this is the biggest cause of today's unhappy world.

The reality is that all experience of life is internal, hence if you don't like anyone or anything, you have to change your mind. Simply because there isn't really an out there which can change. There are just myriad perspectives of the same happenings or persons.

Change comes from changing our own perspective; it comes from within. Real change comes when you drop all perspectives and adapt the universal perspective of respect for life.

We have to understand and realise that the experiencer of all life is one, as all life is a product of your thoughts and thinking. Hence, if the story running in your mind is not stable and in peace, the world will never be in peace for you.

Now we have to agree that the story in everyone's mind has to be stable for the shared human reality to be peaceful and full of love.

For this, we have to remove the veil of our perspective and thinking to see beyond that. Understand that all perspectives are good in their own way, but as long as the strong duality of "I" and "You" remains, there will never be peace within or with-out us.

This has been the message behind all philosophies and religions of the world today. Most called this shared conscious experience: GOD.

Today our social, legal, family, education and cultural systems are built on the dual world of thinking and difference in perspectives. Today, it is "I" against "You". Mine versus yours.

We have forgotten, that we roamed the earth together thousands of years ago to find water and food to build a society. In this society, slowly, the roles we assumed became our personality and individualism was born. Over time, a social structure has evolved which has the acquisition and growth of money as a core objective. We humans have forgotten that money is a means of transaction and not something one can acquire.

Chasing money and living for the future is against the very nature of humans and our way of living. Hence widespread unhappiness is experienced in society today.

However, many of us are waking up to seeking the nature of reality as the human brain has developed enough to ask this question. We have also reached a point where our lives are dependent on medicine, which is addictive in nature, and we have adopted a human lifestyle which is lethargic and lazy. Ask yourself, is this how life is supposed to be?

It is time for us to fight the system, by fighting our own habits and building a new experience of life that respects all life. It is time for the evolution of thought and the human experience. It is time to rediscover what we lost; a lifestyle and understanding of reality that is holistic and focuses on the real experience of life instead of the story and drama of life.

After years of addictive programming of the brain by social media, reality TV, money, excessive consumption, culture, values, history, fake news, politics, excessive work, eternal quest growth, spiritual seeking, medicine abuse, food toxins and so on, we need a reset of the brain and body.

With Logical Humanism, I attempt to provide a modern, logical and scientific understanding to claiming your brain and body back from the thinking person and hence the society, so you can do what you came here to do: live and love.

I believe it's how we humans will evolve and cope with this changing nature of the world, climate, advancing AI and rising cost of living.

Leaders of tomorrow will understand the nature of their beings and the working of their brains, and by that also realise our society's addictive and limited behaviour. Politicians, leaders, musicians, artists, writers, entrepreneurs, changemakers and lovers of tomorrow will change the core of the social system by changing the base conditioning of their own brains.

We all desire a radical and fundamental change, however, it starts by understanding the nature of what you call "I am". The work starts within us.

Thank you for reading.

Sebastian Lyall

Author Bio

Sebastian is an ex-journalist and a serial entrepreneur from London, United Kingdom. His journey from a very successful journalist, financier, trader, and businessman, to a clinically depressed, suicidal person on myriad pills and then to the person who is writing this book, is full of learnings and insights. Since his sudden awakening experience, hundreds of people have met him during his travels and journeys across the world, where this seed was planted into their brains. Many have conversed with him about the concepts discussed and have followed this path of least resistance.

The understanding of this concept is growing fast as the world is going through a fundamental shift, leading to events which can shape the evolutionary path of humans in the time of AI, war, inflation, mass migration, mental health epidemic and climate change.

Sebastian designed immersive experiences for a living before he started writing this book. His creations are well-known across the globe, including the world's first naked restaurant. He has been talked about, and interviewed, by celebrities like Ellen de Generes, and his creations are covered by all major publications of the world including BBC, Forbes, NY Times, Wall Street Journal, El Mondo, La Monde and Washington Times. Sebastian was also named the "Most Innovative Entertainment CEO in 2022" and Forbes called him a "Maestro"

Before his last venture, he was a technology entrepreneur and a commodities trader at various banks and hedge funds. His professional career in

London, New York, Paris and many other cities spans over 20 years.

His work made him study human psychology and anthropology in an attempt to identify and shape possible shifts in culture and society. He learned all human demands and desires are rooted in the experiences and data of the past, thus creating an addictive, compulsive and unhappy human body and mind. This human mind has created a society which is not in line with reality and its nature.

Over the years of communicating and interacting with younger people, he came to learn about their psyche and trained himself in storytelling to this generation. He spoke at conferences all over the world about this understanding in the context of experiences and hospitality.

He pioneered a new industry within the service sector called "Immersive Hospitality", combining interaction and activity with food and beverage. He brought the realisation to the industry that immersion enables a normal going-out experience to have a very different impact on people's brains and hence lives.

Having experienced and seen reality first-hand, following a life-altering surgery and subsequent depression and suicide attempts, Sebastian left his Ferraris, businesses, relationships and all his life back in London in search of an answer. Why aren't we happy and how can we end pain and suffering?

He travelled to Greece, Italy and Thailand and met many people on the way, who understood and connected with this message.

His life mission now is to make people realise "what" they are, as opposed to the person they think they are. He believes this understanding and a lifestyle of least friction that embodies stillness can bring a huge shift and peace to personal lives, and society as a whole.

This journey, which started 6 years ago after his surgery, includes over 2000 hours of training, practice of stillness, breathing and movement work. This routine continues as he meets and teaches many fascinating people along the way.

As a successful experience designer and cultural anthropologist, Sebastian brings a unique perspective to the exploration of inner peace and reality with a modern approach.

Through logical analysis, introspection, and relatable storytelling, Sebastian seeks to inspire readers to question their own perceptions, embrace their true selves, and experience life beyond the limitations of the mind to find ultimate peace and joy.

Printed in Great Britain
by Amazon

38026617R00106